THE ANATOMY OF STRUCTURES

THE ANATOMY OF STRUCTURES

Rebecca Goss

For Angela,

Happy birthday to you!

With best wishes,

Rebecca Goss

March 2013

FlambardPress

First published in Great Britain in 2010 by Flambard Press Ltd
Holy Jesus Hospital, City Road, Newcastle upon Tyne NE1 2AS
www.flambardpress.co.uk

Reprinted 2010

Typeset by BookType
Front cover print: 'Great Expectations' by Charlotte Hardy
Author photograph by Rosie Bennett
Cover Design by Gainford Design Associates
Printed in Great Britain by Bell & Bain, Glasgow, Scotland

A CIP catalogue record for this book is available from the British Library.

ISBN: 978-1-906601-17-1

Flambard Press wishes to thank Arts Council England
for its financial support.

Flambard Press is a member of Inpress.

The paper used in this book is FSC accredited.

Jim, Jamie, Rosie, Ella, Jack

'Near and far, near and far,
I am happy where you are'

Ogden Nash

Contents

A Man Greets His Wife from Her Short Break Away

The first thing they do is embrace.
Fat smiles stay on their faces
all the way to the restaurant.

He eats ribs with sticky, podgy fingers.
She bites chicken wings with shiny lips.
They have a pudding each and share another.

In the car, she tells him about a girl she saw,
with a short, spotted skirt that flapped
around one long limb.

'There wasn't even a stump to satisfy me,
just a space where the leg should've been.'
'Was she very pretty?'

'Yes she was.'
They stop talking and at traffic lights
he strokes her thigh, instead of saying

how sad her story sounds. Quietly, he resents the one-legged girl
for changing the mood between them, resents his wife
for telling him the tale at all.

Making love to her later, it's a pretty teenager
sitting astride his wide belly. One leg tucked behind,
leaving the torso, smooth and deformed, moving over him.

Burgle Me

Living alone and imagining burglary,
she never once envisaged violence.

In her premonitions, she would return to find
her usual force on the front door

blocked by the chain, rear gate swinging,
bike gone, an inevitable puddle of glass.

When it happened, she was kicked into the kitchen.
Tape yanked around her ankles,

she lay like a bound piece of game,
watching them search, empty, steal.

One of them leant close,
did something terrible to her eye.

Months later, drunk at a wedding,
she danced, smiled for photographs.

A guest admired the boldness of her pose,
the slit in her skirt, longed to tuck his nails

beneath her eye patch, lift it at the edges
and right there, in front of everyone, steal a look.

Treasures

Seven months after they made you redundant,
I found a parcel of raw meat at the bottom of the wardrobe.
Blood had begun to sweat through layers of paper,

staining your shoes and mine. My summer ones,
with stretch of white gauze and sexy satin heel,
absorbing that dazzling spread. No bad smell,

you must have only just put it there, my peculiar gift.
You dressed, got a bus, went out and paid for it,
let the finest scotch beef swing in a bag at your shins.

Heavy with time, you didn't embrace redundancy
with cooking, or woodwork or pills.
You just hid things, small moments of evidence

that you left your chair when I wasn't there.
I stopped shouting at you, eager for more treasures
and though we never say a word about it,

I still lift second-hand books from the washing,
take soap bars from coat pockets,
stroke the new white hairs on your head while you sleep.

Labor Day, Long Island

My girlfriend was sipping his pink lemonade,
laughing as if she really didn't know
he wanted to touch her.

His repeated invitation
to 'cocktails on the yacht'
were words that gently tugged
at my girlfriend's common sense.

She leaned to bite my shoulder,
whispered 'Why not?'
I stared at the rings on his toes. Glistening
blue and silver, on fat golden stubs.

Pigeon Love

I know he sweats in his bed about me.
Nights before races are longest,
as he dreams of the money my feathers
can make him, sees my eager beak pointing

towards home. Nights like this are hard for me too,
caging us together, my love and I,
leaving me to nudge her plumy neck,
peck that secret part beneath her wing.

He relies on *widowhood* to get me back,
simple but it works. Passion, sex, comfort
being parted from all that, makes me fly faster,
guarantees I'm a winner. When that businessman

in Taiwan bet $50,000, did he know he wagered
on mourning and love? At six days old, they punched
a ring on my leg, the number defining my lot,
who I belonged to and he does care for me –

pets me with chubby, tender hands
but she's the one who increases my rapidity,
her softness accelerates swiftness,
lift up your wing, high so I can see, I'm coming home.

widowhood: term used to describe the period racing pigeons
spend apart from their mate during flights.

Jealousy

She wakes, he watches her walk to the landing,
knows she is pushing open their son's door,
waiting for the regular lift of his chest.

She will now brush her teeth,
that curious late-night habit, come back to him,
the sting of toothpaste in her mouth.

They wait for the heaviness of sleep.
He wants her hair in his face, sweat on her neck,
the child watching them, from the end of the bed.

Wants the boy to see him being held tight,
fucked into existence, wants his wife to understand
why he wakes every morning, clutching her arm or hip,

some part of her, to stop himself
from slipping in his night sweat, losing her forever.

Stopping Distance

She threw her wedding ring into the long grass
of their garden two years after he died.

In the night, desperate with a heavy torch,
she clawed at the damp ground, sobbing.

Her mother suggested cutting up his shirts
to use for dusters. She took an afternoon off work,

piled the shades of Egyptian cotton at her feet.
Slicing away the arms, she began to fillet large squares

of cloth, smoothing them flat on the kitchen table.
A patchwork of arguments, dinner parties, sex

spread before her. A story for each shirt,
but the pale blue Ralph Lauren bought for his thirtieth

was missing. He wore it that day, getting into the car,
the sun causing him to narrow his eyes as he waved

leaning from the window, promising to call her when he got there.

Leotard

He comes across it by accident.
His washing pile muddled with hers.
It's slippery, black, has a nice stretch to it.

There's a mirror, an empty flat,
so he strips, feels goose bumps spread
the back of his thighs. He pulls it up too fast,

has to re-tuck his balls inside the narrow gusset.
Once on, tight and shiny, he distorts his physique
with high-arm stretches. The cat purrs approvingly

from the edge of the bed. One last glance,
Lycra wrapping the round of each buttock,
he inhales and exhales, gets ready to leap.

Her Things

Every time I sit and piss in your bathroom
I don't stare at my toes or pale hairs on my thigh,
I stare at the shelf above the radiator.
Cacharel perfume, Clinique toner No.1,
a glass jar of cotton-wool pads, razors, dust.
Wrapped soaps from hotels, Clarins freebies,
a deep jar of moisturiser, that I opened once,
saw the fossilised swipes of her fingers.

Eventually, I ask if we can move it all.
You are frowning, quizzical. I pull on your arm,
lead you upstairs to look at the shelf
where we realise her belongings have morphed
into mine. Untouched for so long they were invisible,
now a woman breathes again in this house
and you thought I had placed my things there,
that I had unpacked them, that I was staying.

Hi Honey, I'm Home

Two soft packets of Marlboro on the sideboard
and she knew he'd arrived.
She lit one, moved to the table
and saw SURPRISE written in spilt sugar.
She couldn't help thinking of flies.
He was in bed for certain, waiting for her
to join him in pseudo-sleep.
Thinking of his mouth, she almost went upstairs,
but telephoned her sister
and arranged to meet in a Tapas bar.
She added D and a question mark
to his greeting on the table,
picked up his cigarettes
and left the front door open.

In the Garden

My trowel spoons out marbles, three muddy
eyeballs, each with its curve of yellow iris.
I wipe them clean, let them clink in my palm,

imagine my house with children in – the marbles'
journey from bedroom, to pocket, to garden,
to ground. I push them back into the wet dark,

dud bulbs for worms to pull blindly
into sockets of soil, their squirming lengths
expecting them to rot or take root.

Mapping

Six days after your discharge,
they are still there, tattoos from the hospital,
water resistant on your upper arm.

Not hearts or daggers, no branded display
of belonging but a big, black arrow
felt tipped onto hurting flesh.

Following its point leads to your shoulder
where the pen has swept over skin
in a practised curve, stopped to dot

around your weakened clavicle.
Simple directions, such basic planning
for the attack. I was at home, eating

on my own, when they pricked a hole
in your bluest vein, let your body slump
and mapped this route into you, while you slept.

Knowledge

'A population study in Sweden indicated that being born lower in sibling order was associated with greater suicidal tendencies in later life.'
The Times, 24 September 2004

The dangerous pull of adulthood comes into our house,
my last child leaves me with this terrifying knowledge.
As he packs cases, gathers his bedroom in armfuls,

I dream about how he will be found. Boots with laces dangling
in a garage, his own children playing outside until it gets dark.
Maybe he will wait, do it after I'm dead, stand for a long time

at a luring river's edge. From now on he will wake and breathe
in rooms I've never seen, move between seasons, women, traffic,
leaving me powerless to plot his stretch before departure.

21

The Anatomy of Structures

for Jim

Discover my signs of historical movement,
scars, faint bruises, a new freckle perhaps.

A mixture of hollow and solid construction
lies beneath these fatty layers.

Rest over my left-hand side, front facing,
what's buried there? My veins tied together,

the fragile suspended timbers of my bones.
Can you see the internal partitions,

parts of my heart divided for our children, for you?
A building pathologist, seeking causes of collapse

could look at my face, find no signs of distress.
So much extensive repair here, the slow digging out

of our histories, we have filled the cavities of loss
and built this new structure of marriage.

Mrs Quigley and I

We bumped into each other
in a department store,
were screwing in her car an hour later.
Continued to do so for weeks, months,
every delicious opportunity we could get.

But yesterday was strange.
She came to me, the morning's rain still caught
in the waxy creases of her coat,
little glass bubbles I wanted to reach out and collect.

She'd found Mr Quigley in the hall,
manic, seething, rattling a dice in its shaker.
He let it roll across the floor, it almost touched her shoes.
'1, 2 or 3, you stay, 4, 5 or 6, you go. Shout out the number!'
He rolled a dice for me, can you believe that?

I loved Mrs Quigley's body,
her breasts, lips, legs. And I liked it married.
Liked covering her with my fingerprints,
so he could wipe them away with his own.

Did you hear that? He rolled a dice for me!
She dropped her shaking head,
the hair dark and damp at her neck.
I touched it lightly, lowered my voice to a lover's whisper,
tell me the number, I said.

Ritual

for Jamie

The tired, stretched V-neck of a school jumper,
struggling to survive another term, lies with washing
at my feet. Cigarette smoke seeps from the weave

of a teenager's jeans. Grey socks, pulled off into balls,
lurk in the pile like stinking dead mice.
My daughter's last nosebleed, so heavy it frightened her,

clots inside a square of scrunched cotton,
whipped from her father's pocket just in time.
Tea towels harbour finger wipes of raw chicken,

bolognaise sauce. The dog's blanket, hairy
and still warm. Odd perhaps, to be fond of this ritual,
ankle deep in the compost of my family.

Discovery

'The prettiest woman I ever kissed was another man's wife,
my dear mother 1941–2005.'
    Tattoo on man's back, Liverpool, summer 2006.

Undiscovered last night, the tattoo is obvious now.
Morning lets me see what I traced blindly in sweat,
affords me clear view its inky crawl across tight,
tanned skin. Black curling loops at the base of your back,
the spot I made arch when I locked my ankles there.
And just as unease shudders over me, a slow turning
in my throat, you wake, roll over, whisper what you want.
I tentatively finger the deep ridge of your spine,
aware that I will find it, like Braille.

After Work

i.m. Mike and Lyndy Clegg

Carriages now rid of commuter weight, the train pulls into sidings
and you become visible. One last shunt makes you roll slightly.

No one found you until they were clearing litter. All those living people,
filling the train with bags, coats, breath, while you lost yours, after work,

after burying your wife some months before. I hope someone tells the man
who found you that you were a widower, that you shaved off the moustache

you'd worn for decades that morning. (Your sister didn't recognise you
on the slab.) So when he finds you again in uncomfortable dreams,

sees the tiny globes of sweat on your smooth upper lip, he can sleep on,
knowing you had started the day with a bold, new face.

Growing

Aged nine, lost in holiday bliss, following his father everywhere,
our son ran two steps too late into the lift, the doors closing
to rip off his arm. We never speak of the blood or foreign sound

that was my husband screaming. He continues to nurture,
but the gentle boasting about his beautiful boy has stopped.
My husband had to bury all that ambition. Every night he sits

on our son's bed, his fingers travelling the stump edge,
searching for a join, wishing a limb to grow quietly in the dark,
so one day, you notice it is longer, as you would his hair, or nails.

Restless

A new text message shivers
inside her pocket, reading it
makes her flushed, tremulous.

Harmless messages, not even
very personal, but in the safety
of her head, she has stepped off trains

to meet him, disappeared into the city,
late sun warming her deceitful back.
She has imagined his breath

on her spine, the hair getting wet
at her temples, gasps coming rapidly
from her open mouth. When asked

what she is thinking she says
the children, or the weekend,
lets her husband kiss her, his tongue

like litmus paper in her nervous mouth,
waits for the lies to be discovered, as they secrete.

Keeping Houston Time

When they were told their son had died,
in a car, in America, he went into the greenhouse
and dismembered a dead bird.
He lay pieces out on a spade,
with splinters of beak around its head
like some gruesome halo.
When she came to the doorway
he looked up from his homemade angel
and with a candour that rarely came easily
said he'd never loved his boy enough.
She looked at her watch, keeping Houston time,
and worked out he'd died while she was sleeping.
'He died while we were sleeping, Jack,'
were the only words she could say to him.

Candour

Moulding my back into the headboard,
I look down at my sleeping wife, push a finger

into her fleshy arm. I watch it sink in, like a child's finger
lost in forbidden icing. With my whole palm, I roll her arm

like a baker's pin, but still can't drag her from the dark.
Shaking a shoulder makes her eyelids spark open.

She sits up quickly, unaware one breast has fallen
from her nightdress. Yawning, her sticky mouth stretches,

sour breath rises in the slim space between us
and I tell her I feel sunken, unloved.

Green Fingers

Every year his Christmas wreath is stolen.
He accused a boy once,
who sniggered and spat at his shoes.

This December, he winds in extra ivy,
laces bitter greens with mistletoe.
His pinched fingers working hard
to make this wreath the most breathtaking.
He nails it to his door at five o'clock,
by six, it is gone.

In his shed, he screws lids on tight,
puts bottles back up high.
He sweeps cuttings into a bag,
knowing they've taken something
more than the prick of holly.
That they're touching it now,
they are breathing it now.

Girl on a Bicycle

She brakes
to watch the prostitutes.

Lies a flip-flop
flat on the ground,

lets the cool pipe
of bike frame

rest against her thigh.
She gawps

at their struts and flicks,
how they shimmy

their skin
as the sun licks it.

She twists her necklace;
lifts fat, red beads

absent-mindedly
to her mouth

whilst one
leaves the pavement,

squats knickerless
in a bush,

pisses into litter and soil.

Running

It was almost light when my father walked into the field to find her.
From my window, I watched the faint beam of his torch,

steady, until he started running. When he brought my mother home
she was already undressing. Soon she was naked from the waist down.

Her tight, adult limbs pale and frightening,
as she negotiated the landing towards me.

Her mouth had a new, difficult smell,
she carried a glass bottle, quarter full and sloshing.

I wanted her far away, back out in the field
where the dark could wrap round her, ease her into sleep

until I woke her in the morning. I'd have food in my bag
so we could eat breakfast in the high grass

and she could plait my hair beneath the oak tree,
acorns forming above us in their cups.

Rise

As his toys bump my naked, sleepy limbs,
I feel him pause over my peculiar skin.
His hands hover the series of strange paths

spreading along my back,
find the whirlpools at my shoulders,
deep and swirling down to my breasts.

It was the urn at a baker's tearooms.
Steaming and spitting at my neck
before cracking apart

to melt my teenage body.
Hospital staff brought cold water,
watched as my hands made it bubble in the bowl.

Now my young son traces the twists
like raw white dough stretching over veins
and wakes me with hungry noises.

I pull on a shirt, carry him downstairs
as he breathes against my collar,
feel my skin warm to him, beginning to rise.

A Great Couple of Days

They began at a sticky diner table,
playing spin-the-fork until seven a.m.
She told her secrets easily, while a favourite song
she'd forgotten about cruised inside her head.

Then there was the bloke she couldn't shake off.
He wanted her to understand how 'rare' his shoes were.
When she looked down at his feet
he wasn't wearing any shoes. She had laughed
and he'd laughed harder.

She didn't once taste something she didn't like.
All the mail she got was good mail.
At the pool, she drifted into a teenage boy
with terrifying eyes and beautiful shoulders.

She found a beauty-queen parade, moved like a princess
beside golden floats, until someone caught her arm
and pulled her back into the crowd.

Aeroplanes

I like to think, when the bomb went off,
she slipped from her seat
into the sky, floated for a time
before the body broke apart.
It's difficult to keep her whole.

Now that this package has come
(her things wrapped in plastic)
I worry they were carelessly scooped up.
That I will tear away the wrapping
to find her fingers, loose, like crayons.

Night of the news flash, I sat on the stairs,
absolutely sure she had survived.
I kept my runway of Christmas lights
blinking on the banister for weeks,
but she didn't make it home.

I'd signed for my daughter's things,
went to work, left them untouched in the hall.
Opening my front door now, a stench hovers.
Diesel fuel, instantly thick in my throat,
with the hang of disinfectant behind.

The package mocks me, it's what I've waited for,
but I find it choking, unpleasant.
I lift it to the garden, let the smell seep upwards,
hear the rumble of distant aeroplanes.

Eagerly, I look for her.
The long, hard legs puncturing clouds
as she falls down to me.
My hands getting ready to grab the feet,
pull her safely through the trees.

Coming

Once, I saw chandeliers,
dozens, dripping crystal
the length of a palace corridor
and they stayed there
for the whole ten seconds of it,
maybe less, my breathing
making the finest droplets turn.

Pay Attention

In church, he notices his daughter
has lost weight. The watch slips
on her wrist each time she touches her hair.
As she sings, the flesh at her jaw seems tight.

Pushing her hand into a small back pocket,
she pulls out lip balm. Lips pouting and apart,
she wipes a shiny finger across her mouth,
nudges for his attention, offers the lip balm to him.

Startled, he recognises the gesture
as one his lover often makes, when they're in the car
or walking secretly in woods, their respective lives buried
for an hour, in order to speak, satisfy, touch.

Virginity

Lost in a cramped flat, gas fire on,
Echo and the Bunnymen on low,

I want you back. Taken on the floor,
in five quick stabs, you're someone else's.

It was lonely in the bathroom without you,
where a week of bleeding started, splashed

on to school socks. A clothes horse straddled
the bath, his wife's bras, knickers dripped.

Gone in minutes, my yoke of fifteen years,
discovered at a disco, his fingers tugging

at you in the outside dark. Come back,
for a wedding, for the making of a life.
This time, leave me trembling, absolved.

My Grandma and the Microwave

After years of neglect, its dated, brown bulk looms
on the worktop and intrigues her. She rummages
for Fairy Liquid, lets the dark green syrup pour
from the nozzle, filling a teacup, heats it on high.

The carer comes, cheap magazine poking
from a carrier bag, the smell from the microwave
not yet inviting inquiry. My Grandma rearranges
her nightclothes on cold cooker shelves, is startled

by the microwave's ping, moves to study her reflection
in its thick black glass. Then she hears her guest
turning pages in boredom at the dining-room table.
She prepares a tray, the books of the Bible come in order

from her whispering mouth, as she releases the microwave
door, reaches for the teacup, bubbling over on its saucer.

The Decorator

got strict instructions not to go inside.
He did, for five minutes, while she popped out.
Shoes on their sides, coat on the unmade bed.
Books split open, belts dangling from a chair.

The smell was so clear, as if all she did
was open and close the window.
A stack of loose change
on the bedside table, mostly old five ps.

Lifting one into his hand sent a fine
grey powder to his nose.
He loaded the van, slammed
the front door like she told him to.

Your Father's Ashes

Swaddled in a Tesco bag for a decade
(family dispute), they now nest in the boot
en route to the West Shore, in Llandudno.

We help your mother across rocks
to the sand. Urn tilted above the waves,
you push the lid, let him fall

in bursts of black cloud. He clusters
to grey pearls, your mother sobs.
Weeks later, she'll be in a care home,

this day forgotten. You are almost orphaned
and a new longing for a baby begins to uncoil,
hook itself into my insides and tug.

The Wife Maker

after Blodeuwedd, from the Mabinogion

Little noises of satisfaction slip from his mouth,
as the glorious mass of colour and scent
spreads along his workbench.
He lifts a delicate stem, strokes its velvet bud,
decides to start the body straight away.

Gold moonshine smothers the twine cage
of her limbs. Rare blossoms surround her lily breasts –
two star gazers, pink and open.
Dense heads of meadowsweet
make the cream of her face.
Petal lips, soft as down, quiver beneath his hands.

He takes pleasure in the long legs and arms.
Stops to breathe in her honeysuckle fingers,
drops baby's breath into the pits
of her belly and mouth.
He has lunch before making the secret garden
deep between her legs.

Almost finished, he tuts, parts the moonshine
with three plunging fingers,
makes room for her forgotten heart.
The thistle lodges under twine ribs,
a perfect white globe, with spikes.

Ink

When I get home, there's fish stuffed with warm,
swollen rice, masses of soggy ratatouille
in my favourite bowl. The head and tail

of the fish don't bother me. As a kid,
I got scared it would start thrashing around on the plate.
Now I nuzzle my fork into its gaping fins,
sure the thing is dead.

We eat eagerly, like sex after three days away from you,
can still surprise each other with interesting stories.
For pudding, you puncture a strawberry with my wedding finger.
The proposal stains into my knuckle,

stays there until we shower.
Rare ink that washes down my left hand, left leg,
swirls at our feet – pale, diluted, then gone.

Fold

Eating toast with butter, my son and I
discuss journeys. Where we want to be heading,
right now. I say, predictably, the beach. To the hut,

with doors shabby and open, damp towels hanging
from the steps. My children's hair dripping
over my warm legs, as they come to me for food.

My son says he'd like to be folded, slipped
into an envelope, sent to a castle. The King
would open him up, fold him into a ship, set him

floating around the moat. *Forever?* I ask. *No.*
Until I fill with water, until I sink to the bottom.
It is not until bedtime that I consider what he said.

Towers

You took us blackberry picking.
Your four children with mushroom boxes ready.
I was twelve. The eldest and alarmed at many things,
yet able to concede the absence of my mother.

Walking there, my brothers, eager and racing,
darted between your side and ditch-edges.
And you, in wellies long enough for my whole arm.
The fruits looked dull from road dust,
our smudging fingers made them bright again,
a lick and they sparkled.

I did not feel anyone was missing.
That day my family felt tight.
I imagined my mother in a tower somewhere,
beautiful and hated.

Going home, boys inspected stained tongues.
The youngest, stealing from his box,
couldn't see the dark slick on his cheek.
I struggled to balance my box. It needed two hands
but I wanted one to hold yours.

The Child's Party

He stood by the cooker, the smell
of melting pizza making saliva pool

on his tongue. He watched her greet
each child kindly, guide them by their small

shoulders as they gripped assorted parcels
for the birthday boy. Loose balloons bumped

her bare freckled legs, he felt a longing
that surprised him. He waited until she

unscrewed the lemonade. Fizz spewed
from the plastic neck, making her jump back,

laughing. She asked him to repeat what he said.
So he admitted the affair again, watched her sticky hands

drop down to her sides. Through the doorway,
a clown pulled a flower from his son's ear,

making him squeal. He wondered how long
it would be, before he struggled to remember the boy's

expressions that day, the smell of his blonde, fragile head.

Swimming with Rosie

Stepdaughter, forever explaining
you're not quite mine, yet

I've seen you bloom, change
with unrealised grace.

Wading in, you bob, bounce, lashes dripping
like they used to in the bath,

a place I don't see you anymore,
your body altering in secret.

You splash and grab,
water allowing tactility lost on dry land.

I smooth my stomach, want to tell you
there's someone here with us, diving its own pool,

developing that blood link between us,
who might swim like you, be like you.

The Escapologist

We've had the shedding of the cape,
the tightening of straps
now begins the squirming,

twisting, until she is thrashing for her life,
a terrified hooked fish, wild
but with one arm freed, now two.

How we cheer the brave escapologist
as they pull her from the sloshing tank.
I feel inside my pocket, my front-row ticket

warm and flat against the lining. Smiling,
I excuse myself from the lions, leave to see
the caravans circled on the grass,

imagine her long naked body
parading the carpet, dripping, triumphant.

Appetite

I am bereaved. I have lost my best friends.
Those cigarettes, each stuffed, rolled
delicacy, sustained me like meat.

Thoughts of meals were stifled
with every smoky mouthful.
While friends perused menus,

I chose another fragile stalk,
brought it to my lips, pleasurable
as any buttery asparagus tip.

People's enthusiasm for my 'new found
taste buds' is nauseating. Covetous
of twenty Camel in someone's hand,

the roof of my mouth drips. It's lunchtime.
I face a sandwich. Complicated layers alien
to my tongue. My doctor insists there is food

in my cupboards. Lists his favourite lunches,
hoping to infect me with an appetite,
but he can't explain the hunger or the grief.

24 hrs

When they said it was over
and we could go home,
my mother wouldn't leave him.
I watched her body
fold around his
and a new pulse
quickened behind my eyes.

In the car she said
he was your brother and you haven't cried.
She got out at his flat
to smell the clothes he wore yesterday.

I wasn't ready for his voice on my machine.
It came at me, a series of fast
demanding sounds,
and punched out all my breath.

Loco Motion

Said he was a painter,
that he'd always wanted to paint
the naked female form
hanging upside down.

We went to a hotel room.
I got a little crazy
on my first whisky,
started dancing
making him do it too,
so we were turning
and shaking, both of us
naked
and screaming.

'D'you think you'd hang for me darlin'?'
We were on the floor, gasping
at the really high ceiling.
I turned my face towards him,
'Bet your life.'

Dogs and Babies

Bathing is tricky, her legs can't hurdle the sides,
stretch easily in the bubbles like they used to.
Instead she's balanced in a plastic chair,

lowered carefully as an egg into warm rolling water.
Dressing is supervised. She pushes shoes on,
doesn't notice her name, in biro, on each tongue.

Downstairs, the day is punctuated with food,
television, circles of conversation until someone
brings in a dog or a baby and suddenly

she's talking about the family Dalmatian
killing itself by leaping from an upstairs window.
The names of her nine siblings come fast and lucid

from her mouth. She knows her mother's hair
was waist length, deep black. Knows the diamonds
in her engagement ring came back from Egypt

in Tom's pocket, but has forgotten about her tights,
stuffed behind the headboard in her room, hoarded, secret, safe.

Baggage

He abandoned his family
(including in-laws) at the airport lounge,
went in search of crisps, sweets,
chanting a list of requested favourites.
In the queue, Coke under each arm,
Mini Cheddars swinging from his mouth,
he juggled for change, caught sight
of two red-headed women – both fat,
desirable and obviously mocking him.

Closer

Leave the dough to prove, you say,
you want to take my photograph.
Persuaded, I strip naked
to the waist, stroll amongst things
we have planted, new colours swarm,
scents rise, I hear the click of your lens,
feel you getting closer. When the children
return from school, I hand out warm bread,
see your camera resting on the worktop,
our secret afternoon coiled in its cool, dark centre.

Sonnet for Clare

We walked across the hospital car park,
nightly, for the whole of winter. I held
your arm, watched our cold breath cloud in the dark,
wondered what we could face tonight, startled
still by her weight, the rings getting bigger
on her fingers. Ward 2X, the Chaplain
had left leaflets, offered to deliver
her from evil, yet we heard the wailing,
smelt the shit in her bed, saw windows fixed
shut with surgical tape. We pull our chairs
close, routinely make her drink, break biscuits
in half and for that small time with her, share
the burden of telling stories that she
treasures, but forgets in seconds, nightly.

Memory

Compost steams, demanding
a trek through apple trees

to leave offerings of peel and skin.
Joining its quiet, quivering rot

a fox lies close to the heap,
his middle dipped with decay.

All the fine things about him:
whisker detail, eyeballs,

shiny snout are long gone.
He is a black slimy pond

with claws. My brother bounds
into this fug of the dead

grapples me to fight
within feet of sludgy remains,

refusing to admit the stench
in his nose, later, when we eat.

Bastille Day Crowd

The nudging was firm, eager, I felt a thumb
tour and press. A hand cupped curves
of denim, long nails fingered the belt at my waist.
I turned, saw a man older than my parents,
when I pleaded 'Stop', he said 'Ah, Anglaise'.
A stranger lifted me as I sobbed into air, called
to my pen pal, arms outstretched to get me,
was delivered back to her in my dirty flesh.

Grandpa Lived in a Caravan

Sepia pictures of American Indians, cut out of books
were pinned to the walls. I found tobacco,
spilt and drying on every yellow surface.
I'd rub it in my palm, take his smell home with me.

Weekday nights, it was TV until Mum came.
Saturdays, it was lemonade and cards.
He dealt like he was sharing gold,
made sure I left a slightly better cheat each time.

And this was all okay, until one weekend, mid-game,
he tore up the pack, lunged, the sun sparking
on his watch as he struck my mouth,
his heart already weakening with confusion and guilt.

Gift

She caught her hair
on his button.
Left strands, long and curling
against his coat
and like a curious child
he followed her through London.

When side by side
waiting
for pauses in traffic,
he twisted her fine threads
and said nothing.

Mr K-W's Pool

for Rebecca Goodchild

The school bus dropped us at the top of the drive.
Three hundred yards down, what we'd been waiting for,
cool, sparkling and ours 'til seven o'clock.

Rucksacks thrown into grass, five of us hurried
out of uniform, impatient to rid the smell of school
and heat. Shyness of P.E. changing rooms lost here,

clothes abandoned, the bold curves of our bodies shone.
We'd only just discovered sex, but felt safer, more desirable
with each other here, as we grabbed, ducked and shouted,

the water blue and luscious in our mouths.
Standing on the edge, ready to dive, I could see the house,
huge and stone grey with a hundred windows.

I imagined him in a room that hadn't yet decayed, his large,
fierce face above a red polka-dot tie. That eye patch.
We never saw him that summer, or thanked him to his face,
only left our hairs, tangled and glistening on his pool-house floor.

Looking at a Dead Man's Things

Men bring out armchairs, singed covers flapping
in the sooty breeze. Like a peculiar garage sale,

his charred possessions spread across the lawn.
The mattress is a struggle with its pool

of fireman's water. She pictures him in bed
when it started, head on one side, smoke stealing

into his nose. Scanning the grass, she sees
shoes – a row of polished, paired survivors.

When she gets there, her father makes tea
for his generous daughter. She scrapes soot

from fingernails while he tunes in the radio and dances,
laughing at the taps of his new, brown brogues.

Host

Ice cubes bob in the punch like shipwrecked luggage,
a salmon lies pink and sacrificial on its cucumber bed.
Candles line the route of arrival, we welcome

old friends into our home. You move amongst women,
leave your hand on their spines and thoughts in my head.
Stranded with the canapés, I bump between couples,

let the tray tilt long enough to allow one blini each.
Retreating to the kitchen, a fox bolts the garden,
flooding the lawn and my husband with security light.

His new friend leans against the bark of our oldest oak,
her small, dark nipple clasped in his hot, furtive mouth.

Poisoned Embroidery

I like the idea of deadly threads
fingered appreciatively by Grandma.
Cushions puffed and lodged
behind a traitor's head.
Some lethal detail
on that bitch's wedding dress.
The ex, who sneered at my aged hobby,
gets his shirts back, ironed
with brand new buttons.

You, Genius

after 'Room in New York' (1932) by Edward Hopper

Did your
academic day
involve
sucking the flesh
from
one pear,
feeling the
juice
       s
         l
           i
             d
               e

to your elbow?

I am waiting
for you to put
down
that paper
and watch me
take off this dress.

Pin-Up

after 'Pin-Up 1963 – For Francis Bacon' (1963) by Sam Walsh

Plum-like, your eye swells a fleshy
murky purple, that will soon bruise gold.

Lips remain smooth, neat,
the dark crack between them

harbouring exotic smells.
Did someone pincer

a mussel from its shell,
drop it in your mouth

as you waited, a hungry gull?
Did they whisper into thick

sticky roots of your hair
things to make you forget me?

Unsettled by such swagger, did jealous fists
cause your cheeks to marble so?

Sway close to me, let me draw
the night's adventures from your face.

At the Butcher's

after 'Meat Painting II – In Memoriam Rene Margritte'
(1967) by Adrian Henri

Body bent, I journey
the glass display,

pause at kidneys,
blood-filled stones

gleaming like unctuous
jewels. Shiny cuts

veined with maps of fat,
invite me to tour each wet

and heavy tray. Eventually
a chop is lifted, bleeding

watery pink juices
into an experienced palm,

lain gently as a newborn
on waiting scales,

ready to be swaddled
in waxy gingham wrap.

Traveller

When
you were weeks old,
secret, budding in the blackness,
I swam in chilly holiday waves, gorged
cake on beach-hut steps, salty drips on my
neck. The day you took hold, started to make
me sick, a summer storm sent us rushing inside,
you were ready to travel the seasons. There for my
birthday, garden busy with dancing, your grainy image
proud on the fridge. We pulled the patchwork blanket from
the cupboard late autumn, felt you throb and dive beneath it.
By Christmas, uninvited hands smoothed your roundness.
New Year brought two funerals. One, saw ninety-three
years celebrated in a boozy London kitchen. The other
came too early. As I cried into your father's shoulder
you kicked me for an hour, small syncopated
punches, assuring me that like spring,
pushing through snow in the remote
Welsh churchyard, you were
coming.

Acknowledgements

Some poems in this collection first appeared in my pamphlet *Keeping Houston Time*, published by Slow Dancer Press in 1997.

Thanks are due to the editors of the following publications, in which some of these poems appeared: *Agenda Broadsheets, Ambit, Chimera Magazine, Equinox, Magma, Mslexia, Orbis, Other Poetry, Parameter Magazine, Seam, Smiths Knoll, Smoke, Stand, The Bow-Wow Shop, The Interpreter's House, The New Writer, The Reader, The Red Wheelbarrow* and *14 Magazine.*

'At the Butcher's' and 'Pin-Up' were first published in *The Poet's Perspective: Poems for paintings in the Walker Art Gallery, Liverpool*, Headland Publications, 2009.

'Host' and 'Discovery' were first published in *In the Telling*, ed. Gail Ashton and Sue Richardson, Cinnamon Press, 2009.

'Growing' and 'Sonnet for Clare' were both shortlisted for the Writers-of-the-Year Competition, 2008 (writers inc).

'Her Things' was shortlisted for the Writers-of-the-Year Competition, 2007 (writers inc).

'Pigeon Love' was Highly Commended in the Mirehouse/Way with Words Poetry Competition, 2007.

'Rise' was first published in the Ragged Raven Press competition anthology *Writing on Water*, 2005.

'The Wife Maker' was first published in *Blodewedd: An anthology*, ed. Edmund Cusick, Headland Publications, 2001.

'Aeroplanes' was a prize-winning poem in The Bridport Prize 2000 and published in the competition anthology.

'Green Fingers' was shortlisted for The Frogmore Poetry Prize 2000 and published in the competition issue of *The Frogmore Papers*.

Several of these poems were successful in *The New Writer* Prose and Poetry Prizes (Collection category) winning 3rd prize in 2006, 2nd prize in 2007 and Highly Commended in 2008.

I would like to thank Will Mackie and Peter Lewis of Flambard Press and John Harvey.